The
True
God

by
Betty Miller

First Edition Published 1980
Second Printing 1982
Third Printing 1983
Fourth Printing 1984
Fifth Printing 1987
Sixth Printing 1988
Seventh Printing 1989
Eighth Printing 1991
Ninth Printing 1994
Tenth Printing 2003
Print On Demand

The True God

ISBN 1-57149-002-7

CHRIST UNLIMITED MINISTRIES, INC.
Pastor R.S. "Bud" Miller - Publisher
P.O. Box 850
Dewey, Arizona 86327

Contents

Preface

Greetings in the name of our Lord Jesus Christ:

I present this book to the body of Christ as the Holy Spirit presented it to me. I challenge you to allow God's Spirit of truth, and the Bible, to test the accuracy of the words within these pages. This book, part of the Overcoming Life Series, is also addressed to all seekers of truth who know not THE CHRIST UNLIMITED, as it would be my privilege to introduce you to Him.

During the early years of the ministry, I struggled to learn how to hear the voice of God. Once, while nervously waiting to speak before a large audience, and not being sure on what subject I should speak, I posed to the Lord in prayer this question: "Lord, what am I going to say to all these people?" In my spirit, I heard Him very clearly reply, "Betty, I was hoping you would not say anything, as I really wanted to speak." Yes, He wants to speak through us, as we yield to His Spirit. Submitting to the Lord and the guidance of the Holy Spirit, I found, was not only possible, but the only way He wants us to minister. **For it is not ye that speak, but the Spirit of your Father which speaketh in you (Matthew 10:20).**

This book is a gift from the Holy Spirit. I take no credit for it. If something within these pages blesses you, enlightens you, brings you closer to the Lord, releases you from fear or bondage, or heals or delivers you, then please lift your voice in praise to the precious Savior of our souls, Jesus Christ our Lord! On the other hand, if you find some of these things difficult to receive, hard to understand, or totally heretical from your viewpoint, would you also look to the Lord and ask Him if it could possibly be the truth? With an open and honest heart, will you ask God to change any pre-conceived ideas, and be free from traditions to receive of Him, His truth? His truth always brings freedom, never bondage. **And ye shall know the truth, and the truth shall make you free (John 8:32).**

In walking with the Lord, I have found we must obey the

things we feel He is speaking to us. In my personal life, I used to be fearful of speaking for the Lord because I was so afraid of missing Him and making mistakes. (He, of course, has now delivered me of all my fears. Praise Him!) He encouraged me not to quit because of mistakes when He spoke these words to me: "Betty, if I receive the glory and praise for all the things that are a blessing to people, I also receive the responsibility for your mistakes, as long as you are striving to please me. I am able to make even those work for your good." **And we know that all things work together for good to them that love God, to them who are the called according to his purpose (Romans 8:28).** We serve a wonderful, loving God, who encourages us to follow and obey Him that we might be blessed, and in turn bless others!

This book was written as an act of obedience to the Lord, whom I dearly love. I consider it an honor to write for Him. Years ago, when I was in prayer, the Lord spoke that I was to write a book, but I never felt it was God's timing, nor did I feel the unction or anointing to begin this work until now. Over the past year God has performed a series of miracles to confirm that it is now His time, and has made the arrangements for this to become a reality.

I pray that this book, along with the Overcoming Life Series, may help you learn to walk closer to our Lord, as He is THE CHRIST UNLIMITED!

I am, by His love,
A handmaiden of the Lord,

Betty Miller
February, 1980

If any man will do his will, he shall know of the doctrine, whether it be of God, or whether I speak of myself (John 7:17).

vi

Foreword

It just seemed natural that I would do the foreword on this book since my wife, Betty, and myself, are "one flesh." God, through the Holy Spirit, has given by revelation to Betty many truths of His Word, which have been set forth in this book.

The Lord spoke to Betty about ten years ago that she was to write a book for Him, and that He would arrange the right time and place to write it. Betty simply took this vision and set it aside until God began to "quicken" her spirit to bring it forth. One morning, very early, Betty awakened, and began to write as the Lord dictated to her. In giving her this small initial portion of the book, he showed her how, by submitting to His Spirit, and completely yielding to Him, He would feed to her the message He wanted to share with the body of Christ. He also revealed how quickly and easily it would be completed. The messages that God has given in this Overcoming Life Series are to all who desire to become "overcomers" and be "conformed to the image of His son" (**Romans 8:29**). Our Lord is not satisfied that a person remains a "babe" in Christ, but longs for each "babe" to grow to maturity. He desires that we should strive to become overcomers, live the overcoming life, and claim the promises of the inheritance of all things that are to be given to the overcomers.

I thank God that He has allowed me to share such close love and companionship with Betty. I know that within her heart she has no personal ambitions, no personal ends to achieve. Betty has simply been doing the will of the Father in the writing of this anointed book. May the Lord bless you with this book, as He has blessed us in being a part of His work.

Yours in Christ,

Pastor R.S. "Bud" Miller

He that overcometh shall inherit all things; and I will be his God and he shall be my son (Revelation 21:7).

Credits & Acknowledgments

ALL PRAISE AND CREDIT
GOES TO **THE CHRIST UNLIMITED**!

Truly Christ, the Father, and the Holy Spirit, are to be praised, not only for this book, but for our very lives. His sacrifice on Calvary made it possible to know Him and all the members of God's family.

As with the printing of any book, there are lots of people responsible for the words on these pages, physical words as well as spiritual words. All the people that have ever been a part of my life, all the people that have prayed and supported this ministry, my friends and my family have truly contributed to this work. Special credit should be given to my husband, Bud, whose faithful and loving prayers, encouragement, leadership, and love are a big part of this book. Also, to everyone whose books and articles I've read, to the ministers of the Gospel, whose sermons I've heard, I express my gratitude. For each has contributed, in some measure, to this book. The list is endless, but eternity has the records. So instead of naming individuals on this page and giving them earthly credit, I prefer the Lord Jesus Christ to reward them each as only He can. God bless you all, and may you be surprised as you open up the box that contains your heavenly treasures.

For the Son of man shall come in the glory of his Father with his angels; and then he shall reward every man according to his works (Matthew 16:27).

Introduction

THE TRUE GOD is a book that will show you the character of God, explaining why He does certain things and why it is against His nature to do other things. You will learn to differentiate between the things for which God is responsible and the things for which the devil is responsible. You will also learn about your responsibilities as a Christian.

THE TRUE GOD deals with the lies Satan has circulated against God in an attempt to discredit Him. If believers have a warped image of God it will impair their ability to love and serve Him. Part of this distorted image comes from imperfect relationships with earthly fathers.

The Bible gives us a description of what God looks like and how He responds to us, His creation. In this book we share these truths so that we can have the kind of relationship with our heavenly Father that He desires.

The True God

John 17:3 And this is life eternal, that they might know thee the only true God, and Jesus Christ, whom thou hast sent.

Knowing God

It may be difficult for some of us to believe that we can really know God, yet it is true that we can. What does God look like? When we think of God, what kind of image comes to our mind's eye? Do we see God as some sort of superpower that hits us over the head with a big stick when we have been bad? Or does our image of God seem so ethereal that we cannot even imagine that, as humans, we could possibly see Him?

Perhaps we see God in the flowers, the birds, the blue sky, the tall pine trees and the mountains, and that is God to us. Some may even view Him as a kindly old man with a white beard and robe, sitting on a golden throne someplace out there called heaven. Maybe our position is that it is impossible to see God.

What is the real truth about God? What does He look like? Recently, numerous people, who have died and gone to heaven, have come back to life and returned to give us testimonies of how God appeared to them. Can we really see God?

To answer this question, I want to share with you from my own personal experience. Not only have I seen God, but He is my dearest friend; and as His friend, I want to introduce others to Him. We can see and know Him if we turn to Him with our whole heart. **Jeremiah 24:7 says, And I will give them an heart to know me, that I am the Lord: and they shall be my people, and I will be their God: for they shall return unto me with their whole heart.**

How did I discover Him? Like a lot of other people, I was

1

told about Him. You see He wrote a book--the Bible--and I was given a copy to read. While reading it I discovered that God had a son named Jesus. He sent Him to this world on the greatest mission of all time. The Book He inspired was unlike any book I had ever read. Many things I did not understand, but some of the lines actually seemed to be "alive," and seemed as though someone were speaking directly to me through that Book.

Now after many years of reading the Bible, I am very well acquainted with that "Someone;" He is the Holy Spirit. He has been a real comfort and a tremendous teacher in my life. I found the Bible was written for the very purpose of answering the question posed at the beginning of this section, "What does God look like?" We truly can know what God looks like, and not only that, we can know Him very intimately. By reading His Book, the Bible, we can also find the answers to all of our questions and problems.

The first thing we must realize about God is that He loves us. The book of John in the Bible reveals His love in a very beautiful way. He loves us, He created us, and He has a plan for our lives. It is a very exciting and fulfilling plan, and we can know what that plan is for each of us individually. To understand God's plan, we must read His Word, or guide Book. Most of our problems in understanding God stem from things we have heard other people say about Him. Since there are so many people with so many different ideas, we then end up with a multitude of misconceptions about God.

Here in the United States, we are blessed in that we hear more truth about God than many others throughout the rest of the world. Yet, much of what we hear is still contaminated with man's ideas and traditions. People in many of the foreign lands are seeking to know God, but because they have never read or heard His Word or received Him in their hearts personally, they have devised gods of their own. We see this prevalent in the idolatrous religions of Buddhism, Hinduism, Islam, etc.

If we are going to know God, we must give His Book and His Word the final authority over every issue in our lives. There has to be one way, and one standard for man to follow. Confusion results when one voice is saying, "This is the way," and another says, "No, this is the way." Each man has a different way -- his own way.

The Bible tells us about this in the book of Proverbs. **Proverbs 21:2** says, **Every way of a man is right in his own eyes: but the Lord pondereth the hearts.** In **Proverbs 16:25** we find, **There is a way that seemeth right unto a man, but the end thereof are the ways of death**.

What is the right way to find God? What does God look like?

Perhaps the most simple answer to this question is, "God looks like Jesus." We see God by looking at Jesus. How do we look at Him? We accomplish this by studying the record of His life as recorded in the gospels of Matthew, Mark, Luke and John. **John 14:1-9** records this account of Jesus' words:

Let not your heart be troubled: ye believe in God, believe also in me. In my Father's house are many mansions: if it were not so, I would have told you. I go to prepare a place for you. And if I go and prepare a place for you, I will come again, and receive you unto myself; that where I am, there ye may be also. And whither I go ye know, and the way ye know. Thomas saith unto him, Lord, we know not whither thou goest; and how can we know the way? Jesus saith unto him, I am the way, the truth, and the life: no man cometh unto the Father, but by me. If ye had known me, ye should have known my Father also; and from henceforth ye know him, and have seen him. Philip saith unto him, Lord, shew us the Father, and it sufficeth us. Jesus saith unto him, Have I been so long time with you, and yet hast thou not known me, Philip? he that hath seen me hath seen the Father....

The way to see God is by looking at Jesus. This does not mean to look at His physical appearance because God is Spirit, and He says in **John 4:24** these words: **God is a Spirit: and they that worship him must worship him in spirit and in truth.**

Therefore, we must have spiritual eyes to see God since He is Spirit.

The "Born Again" Experience

How can we receive this eyesight? **John 12:44-46** tells us; **Jesus cried and said, He that believeth on me, believeth not on me, but on him that sent me. And he that seeth me seeth him that sent me. I am come a light into the world, that whosoever believeth on me should not abide in darkness.** If we simply believe on Him and turn from our wickedness with a repentant heart, He saves us and gives us new eyesight. Old things pass away and we become new creatures in Him. We not only are "born again" with a new Father, but within us is the potential to become just like His firstborn Son, Jesus.

John 14:12 goes on to say, **Verily, verily, I say unto you, He that believeth on me, the works that I do shall he do also; and greater works than these shall he do; because I go unto my Father.**

What kind of works was Jesus doing? He went about preaching, teaching, healing the sick, opening blind eyes, opening deaf ears; He performed miracle after miracle. These same works we can do. How can such a thing be possible? This can only be possible through the power of the Holy Spirit.

John 14:13-21 continues: **And whatsoever ye shall ask in my name, that will I do, that the Father may be glorified in the Son. If ye shall ask any thing in my name, I will do it. If ye love me, keep my commandments. And I will pray the Father, and he shall give you another Comforter, that he may abide with you for ever; Even the Spirit of truth; whom the world cannot receive, because it seeth him not, neither knoweth him: but ye know him; for he dwelleth with you, and shall be in you. I will not leave you comfortless: I will come to you. Yet a little while, and the world seeth me no more; but ye see me: because I live, ye shall live also. At that**

day ye shall know that I am in my Father, and ye in me, and I in you. He that hath my commandments, and keepeth them, he it is that loveth me: and he that loveth me shall be loved of my Father, and I will love him, and will manifest myself to him.

John 15:7 gives us the key for becoming like Jesus, **If ye abide in me, and my words abide in you, ye shall ask what ye will, and it shall be done unto you.**

How can we become like Jesus? Very simply, it is accomplished by abiding or fellowshipping with Jesus and keeping His words. That is why Bible study is an imperative part of our walk with God. The Bible reveals to us the nature of God.

The greatest attribute of God is that He is a God of Love. In **I John 4:7-16** we find these words:

Beloved, let us love one another: for love is of God; and every one that loveth is born of God, and knoweth God. He that loveth not knoweth not God; for God is love. In this was manifested the love of God toward us, because that God sent his only begotten Son into the world, that we might live through him. Herein is love, not that we loved God, but that he loved us, and sent his Son to be the propitiation for our sins. Beloved, if God so loved us, we ought also to love one another. No man hath seen God at any time. If we love one another, God dwelleth in us, and his love is perfected in us. Hereby know we that we dwell in him, and he in us, because he hath given us of his Spirit. And we have seen and do testify that the Father sent the Son to be the Saviour of the world. Whosoever shall confess that Jesus is the Son of God, God dwelleth in him, and he in God. And we have known and believed the love that God hath to us. God is love; and he that dwelleth in love dwelleth in God, and God in him.

The kind of love that is mentioned here is not the kind of love that is in the world. God's love is selfless. He gave up His Son that we might live.

In Greek there are three words for love: (1) Love that is divine, called *agape*; (2) Love of high ideals, called *phileo* (our city of Philadelphia is named for this brotherly love); and (3) Love of physical passion, called *eros* (our word *erotic* stems from this word). Since the original text of the New Testament was written in Greek we know the verse above was referring to *agape* love and not the other two. This is evident when we research the Greek manuscripts. (The Old Testament was written in Hebrew with a few passages in Aramaic.)

In studying the Gospels, we find that Jesus died an innocent death on a cross two thousand years ago to pay the penalty for your sins and mine. It was God's great love for us that allowed His Son to suffer death. Jesus conquered sin, death and hell on the cross because He fulfilled the Father's demand for a perfect sacrifice which was an innocent Man without sin. The grave and hell could not hold Him, so He arose victorious and now lives, seated at the right hand of God until the hour for His second coming to this earth. His death and blood atoned for our sins, and if we accept what He has done for us, we need not take the penalty of hell, since He took it for us. Praise God for this sacrifice of love!

John 3:16-18 tells of this love: **For God so loved the world, that he gave his only begotten Son, that whosoever believeth in him should not perish, but have everlasting life. For God sent not his Son into the world to condemn the world; but that the world through him might be saved. He that believeth on him is not condemned: but he that believeth not is condemned already, because he hath not believed in the name of the only begotten Son of God.**

To sum up all the verses I have quoted, we conclude that God cannot be seen physically, but we can look at Jesus and see what He did for us on the cross. We see God's love through the sacrificial death of His Son. When we accept what Jesus did, and turn from our sins, we are then "born again" in the spirit and have new spiritual eyes with which to see God.

What great love to take our punishment upon Himself! He

did not deserve it; He never sinned. It was due to His love for you and me that this great sacrifice was made.

Not only did Jesus make a sacrifice by laying down His life, but the Father bore much grief also. God had to forsake His own Son at His most agonizing moment because He, being Holy, could not look upon sin.

Matthew 27:46 says, **... Jesus cried with a loud voice, saying ... My God, my God, why hast thou forsaken me?** The Father's heart was broken too, as He turned His back on Jesus while He was made to be a sin offering for us. **II Corinthians 5:21** states, **For he hath made him to be sin for us, who knew no sin; that we might be made the righteousness of God in him**.

The Holy Spirit of God was grieved, as He too endured the shame and suffering of the cross. Since Jesus offered Himself **... through the eternal Spirit ... (Hebrews 9:14)**, all the members of the Godhead shared equally in the cost of the amazing plan of redemption. What an act of love! God the Father, loving us; God the Son, loving us; and God the Holy Spirit, loving us. It is difficult for man to realize the agony the blessed Trinity experienced for man.

These past few pages have covered the plan of salvation and the miracle of God, the "new birth." Nicodemus, a man that came to Jesus, did not understand this and asked Jesus what it meant. You can read that story in **John 3**.

Jesus' words in **John 3:6-7** were, **That which is born of the flesh is flesh; and that which is born of the Spirit is spirit. Marvel not that I said unto thee, Ye must be born again.**

When we experience the "new birth" we enter into the kingdom of God as a newborn baby, and we must do certain things so that we can grow spiritually.

Spiritual Growth

The three most important things that hasten our daily growth are daily prayer, Bible study and fellowship with like believers. God does not want us to remain babies, but wants us to grow to maturity in Him. Spiritual growth is not measured in earthly years, as our progression can be rapid or slow depending on our submission and obedience to the Lord.

Another important factor that determines our rate of growth is the keeping of a right heart attitude before Him. We must guard this daily lest a wrong attitude settle in our heart and cause us to break fellowship with God. We must quickly repent and ask God to forgive us so we can resume our relationship.

I John 1:9 says: **If we confess our sins, he is faithful and just to forgive us our sins, and to cleanse us from all unrighteousness.**

One of the most effective devices Satan uses to hinder our growth in God is to send an accident, tragedy, illness, financial crisis, etc., and then blame it on God and convince us that God is chastising us for some wrong. This is a lie of the enemy. Our precious Father loved us so much that He sent His Son to die for our sins and save us. If he gave us His most priceless possession, do you think He would deny us any good thing? No, our God came to redeem us from the curse, not put one on us. Satan is the troublemaker, the robber, the thief, the destroyer and the master liar. Jesus, while on earth, went around doing good, healing the sick, setting the captives free and ministering the message of love.

The Lord chastises us through His Word and by the Spirit. When we do wrong, our spirits are chastised and the Holy Spirit speaks to us of our wrong. We step out of God's will by our own choice, thus leaving ourselves open for an attack of the enemy. This is one way the enemy can gain legal ground to bring his forces upon us.

Ignorance of God's Word is another means by which Satan can put things on us. **Hosea 4:6**, says, **My people are destroyed for lack of knowledge**.

The enemy constantly tries to bring things on us; if we do not know our rights in Christ and resist him, he can succeed. **James**

4:7 says, **Submit yourselves therefore to God. Resist the devil, and he will flee from you.** Satan tries to prevent us from moving forward in the Lord because he knows that when we do, we eventually overcome and defeat him. When we are determined to serve the Lord, then the Lord can take what Satan has meant for evil in our lives and turn it to good. Let us defend the Father and place the blame for evil on Satan where it belongs.

We must get a revelation of who God is and what His will is for us, or we will believe the lies of the devil; and he will destroy our faith. This is the main target of the enemy: our faith. He only uses the problems to get at our faith. He knows if he can destroy our faith in the Lord, he then can destroy us.

Spiritual Eyesight

We need to be able to see God with the eyes of the Spirit to truly know Him. One of our major problems in fellowshipping with the Lord is that we do not know Him as He really is. Therefore, we are not able to serve Him in the way we would like. To be a victorious, overcoming Christian, we need to actually have three revelations: (1) To Know Who God Is; (2) To Know Who We Are; (3) To Know Who We Are In Him or rather to know who He is in us.

First, we must know "Who God Is."

Some people say that no man can see God and live because a portion of Scripture in **Exodus 33:20** that says, **And he (the Lord) said, Thou canst not see my face: for there shall no man see me, and live.** Yet we see that Isaiah **...saw the Lord... (Isaiah 6:1).** Looking at these two verses, there appears to be a contradiction. However, if we ask the Holy Spirit to give us revelation concerning these Scriptures, we discover that they are really not in opposition after all. We only need to view them in the proper perspective and context. This is particularly true of these Scriptures.

Doctrinal error emerges when people take a few Scriptures

9

and build a doctrine on them. Because they are taken out of context, or out of balance, they don't interpret them to mean what the Bible is really portraying.

The proper way to deal with Scripture is to view each portion of the Scripture as a part of the whole. In **2 Corinthians 3:6**, we find this verse, **Who also hath made us able ministers of the new testament; not of the letter, but of the spirit: for the letter killeth, but the spirit giveth life.** An able minister will not take the "letter of the law" and make a doctrine, but will allow the Spirit to reveal each portion of the Scripture as a part of the whole.

Perhaps a better way for us to understand this would be to see that if we took one letter out of a word, we wouldn't have a complete word; or if we took one word out of a sentence, we wouldn't understand the sentence.

The same is true of the Word of God. We should study it in its totality and not isolate one portion of Scripture if we are to get the whole meaning.

To do this we must remember that the great theme and whole message of the Bible is that God loved us and sent a Saviour, Jesus Christ, to die for our sins that we might have life through Him. He came to save us and give us abundant life. If we lose this message in any of our Scriptures, we lose the true identity and knowledge of God. We cannot love, worship and serve a God we cannot know. We must study other portions of God's word that deal with the same subject if we are to get complete light.

Keeping this principle in mind, let us look at our verses in Exodus and Isaiah again. The former verse says, **No man can see God and live,** and the latter, **...I saw also the Lord sitting upon a throne, high and lifted up, and his train filled the temple.** He goes on to say in **Isaiah 6:5, Woe is me! for I am undone; because I am a man of unclean lips, and I dwell in the midst of a people of unclean lips: for mine eyes have seen the King, the Lord of hosts.**

If we spiritually understand this, we will know that any man

10

that really sees God will die. The old creature will die and the new creature will be "born again." If we ever really get a glimpse of God and see Him for who He really is, we will die. Just as Isaiah here had the experience of seeing God, suddenly something else happened; he saw himself. He saw what he looked like and knew who he was -- a man with unclean lips.

We need this same revelation of "Who we are" today. When we come to know the Lord, we find that there is nothing good in us; **...there is none righteous, no, not one (Romans 3:10)**. We see our sin in the light of His holiness. We see our unworthiness, our shame, our guilt; we see our need for the Saviour.

The Beauty of His Holiness

I had an experience with the Lord a number of years ago similar to Isaiah's. This particular experience occurred in the office of my laboratory as I was praying. (Before God called me into a full-time ministry I was in the medical profession. I owned and operated a medical lab and x-ray office.) As I was talking to the Lord, He appeared before me. I saw Jesus' face and immediately was captivated by His eyes. When I looked into them, it was breathtaking. I saw infinite love, divine beauty, gentleness and tender kindness. I saw unlimited authority in those soft eyes! It was wonderful! Words cannot adequately describe all I saw in Him. There isn't any thing or person on this earth that compares with His matchlessness!

My reaction to His presence, I will never forget. I fell down on the floor, just as Isaiah did, and began weeping, thinking of how unclean I was. I felt as if I were a puddle of mud at His feet. I began to cry unto God and say, "Oh Lord, there is nothing good in me. Anything that is good in me is what you have placed there by your Spirit; but there is so much more in my flesh that needs to go, so that you can live in me. Oh Lord, crucify me, let me die, let me die. Let me die to all my ways as I want to live for you. Lord, when I get to heaven, I want to be close to you; just let me be close to you. No matter what must be done in my life here, Jesus, do it so I might be close to you. If I could just wash your feet throughout eternity for the privilege of gazing into your eyes, I would gladly accept that duty. Oh Lord, let me die that I might be close to you!"

From that time on my Christian walk with the Lord has never been the same. I have had such a love for the Lord that my heart's desire has been to serve Him and delight in His will. I know that I could not even have prayed the above prayer except that it was the work of the Holy Spirit within me. Man cannot cry out for death unless God's Spirit enables him to do so.

Sometimes we try to gain favor with God by our works, thinking if we do enough good things we can please Him. It is not our works that will attain a position in God, it's our relationship. Our works come as an overflow of our being with Jesus. As we fellowship with our Father, we begin to take on His nature. We desire that nature when we have seen the beauty of the Father.

I caught a glimpse of that beauty and that is what I wanted, even though I thought, "I am so weak, I could never be like Him. How could I ever attain anything in God, knowing all my faults and failures? It will be too hard; I will be doing good just to get to heaven."

The Lord revealed to me these were thoughts the devil was bringing to my mind, and that it was possible to overcome and walk in victory. Though I was weak, He was strong. I needed that revelation of who I was in Christ or rather who He is in me.

He wanted me to know, **Ye are of God, little children, and have overcome them: because greater is he** (the Holy Spirit) **that is in you, than he** (the devil) **that is in the world (1 John 4:4)**. All He asks us to do is to yield ourselves completely to Him, and He will do the overcoming. He desires us to commit our lives totally, and He will do the changing and the molding. He changes our old natures to His new nature; old desires pass away and we have new desires.

Some people are afraid that if they yield everything to God

they will lose their will and their personality. This is not true. He simply changes our will and our desires and brings our personalities to bloom. We really cannot become all that He intends until we give Him the right to begin that work. He creates within us a new nature.

We sometimes think that walking with God is hard when, in actuality, it is easy. We are the ones that make it hard. We often struggle and try so hard to please God with our good works and attempts to change our old nature, while His way is not difficult at all. **Matthew 11:29-30** says, **Take my yoke upon you, and learn of me; for I am meek and lowly in heart: and ye shall find rest unto your souls. For my yoke is easy, and my burden is light.** By this verse we can see if we are yoked with Him and have ceased to be rebellious to the will of God, we will have an easy walk with Him. The oxen represents a "broken" or tamed animal. We, in our old nature are untamed, but as we yield to the Lord, we will learn "brokenness."

We are so concerned many times that if we go left instead of right, the Lord will be so angry with us and strike us with a big stick for missing Him. Our ideas of God are so warped. He is a beautiful Person and when we are truly trying to please Him, He is not angry with us.

If we think He is a harsh taskmaster, we miss the beauty of loving Him and fellowshipping with Him. If we allow Him to work in our lives, we find that we can overcome all obstacles and every problem the enemy uses to discourage us. In Him, we can do all things. **Philippians 4:13** says, **I can do all things through Christ which strengtheneth me**. If I know who God is, that is, His nature, His power and His love, and if I know that in me there is no good thing (so that I am not tempted to be lifted in pride and take credit for things that should be credited to Jesus), then I also must know that in Him I have all of His power and authority to overcome anything. Praise God for this beautiful truth! We do not need to lead defeated Christian lives, but can walk in victory every day!

It is essential to have these revelations in the proper order, too.

If we discover "Who God is" without the other two revelations, we may have an abnormal view of God. If we find out "who we are" without the knowledge of God, we will not be able to bear it. That is why so many commit suicide. They see themselves and can find no answers within, and therefore see no way out of their problems but to kill themselves. If we discover "who we are in Christ or who Christ is in us" before we get a glimpse of ourselves, we become lifted in pride, soon forgetting that it is not us accomplishing the works of God, but it is the name of Jesus and the power of the Holy Spirit. So we need to make our discovery of God first, ourselves second, and then ourselves in Christ third. With these three revelations we truly can be overcomers.

The Fullness in Christ

The most important discovery we make is to know the Lord and His nature. **Isaiah 9:6** gives us a description of the Lord, **For unto us a child is born, unto us a son is given: and the government shall be upon his shoulder: and his name shall be called Wonderful, Counsellor, The mighty God, The everlasting Father, The Prince of Peace.** In looking at this verse, we can see that He was a child, a son and an adult: Because of this He can identify with each of us at the level that we are presently walking.

We don't serve a God that is so far beyond us that He cannot reach us where we are.

When we are "born again" we become first a baby, then grow to adulthood in a way that is parallel to our natural growth.

Now, because we are all on different growth levels, it does not make us superior members in the body of Christ if we happen to be on a higher level than someone that has just entered the kingdom of God. There are no big "I's" and little "you's" in the body of Christ. The "great" apostles and leaders in the kingdom do not have it over the "little, lowly" saints. We are equal in God's sight and in His love. **Acts 10:34-35** says, **...Of a truth I perceive that God is no respecter of persons: But in every nation he that feareth him, and worketh righteousness, is accepted with him.**

However, there is an advantage that one Christian can have over another, and that is in his knowledge of God's Word and the application of that knowledge in his life. The more of God's Word that one knows and applies, the more victory and power he has.

John 15:7 states, **If ye abide in me, and my words abide in you, ye shall ask what ye will, and it shall be done unto you.** This does not mean that one is superior, but that one has something that another does not have -- more of God's Truth. For example, if someone has been saved, he definitely has something more than those who do not know our Lord. If one Christian has come to experience the baptism in the Holy Spirit, he walks in a power that other Christians do not know. If one knows of the healing power of the Lord, he has an advantage over another who does not know he can receive healing from our precious Lord.

Yes, Christians can have an advantage by knowing God's Word and by applying that Word to their lives and circumstances. But in God's eyes it will not make them more loved or superior to any other member of Christ's body (**1 Corinthians 12:12-27**).

We must realize that each of us is important, and each of us is needed. Each of us has an important place in the body. The devil will whisper to us, "God couldn't use you, who do you think you are?" If we do not recognize his voice, we will not respond to the Lord's call to us. We will think, "Not me, Lord. What could I do?"

One of the highest calls, and the first call we all receive, is the call to intercessory prayer (praying on the behalf of others). We can circle the entire globe through our prayers. We may not go forth physically to the mission field. But we can go by the Spirit through prayer or by furnishing funds for others to go. When we get to heaven, we may be surprised to see some little elderly woman whose rewards will exceed some of the well-know evangelists simply because she has spent many years in the prayer closet.

Some people who are in the forefront now will have to take a back seat in heaven because God looks on the hearts of people, and not on their works. (**Mark 10:31** says, **But many that are first shall be last; and the last first.**) Certainly we must do works for the Lord, but they must be works of the Spirit and not works of the flesh. Works of the Spirit are those works unctioned by the Holy Spirit and these are the only ones that will count toward our heavenly rewards. Remember the Lord's words in **Matthew 7:22-23: Many will say to me in that day, Lord, Lord, have we not prophesied in thy name? and in thy name have cast out devils? and in thy name done many wonderful works? And then I will profess unto them, I never knew you: depart from me, ye that work iniquity.**

When the Lord lays a burden on our hearts and we are faithful to pray and obey the things He is speaking to us, then these works will count. We can gain much through prayer alone. This is one of the most important ministries, if not the most important ministry. Every ministry has its beginnings in intercessory prayer.

As we "walk in the Spirit" and obey the Lord, we accrue rewards in heaven. He then gives us His authority and power on this earth. He gives this authority to us according to the godly character that has grown in our hearts. God cannot give us authority without His character because we would misuse it. Until His image is formed in us, we must be limited in the authority and power we receive from Him. When his nature is formed in us, then He can give us the unlimited anointing because He is THE CHRIST UNLIMITED.

Growth in Christ

God would like for His people to prosper in many things, but in many cases this might mean the ruin of their lives. Maybe they could not handle a lot of money, as the pride of life and the lust for material things would turn them from God. They would be so busy handling the money, they would have no time for God or would "play God" with it. Not having the mind of Christ, they could give it to the wrong people, and it could do more damage than good.

We must be mature enough in Christ to know and recognize the Lord's voice when giving money. Satan is the god of this world and he has the power to influence us so that we give to wrong things, thereby robbing us of putting our money where it would do the most good.

The Lord wants us to grow to maturity so that we come to a place where we have His knowledge and wisdom in every circumstance that faces us. To do this we must learn to make judgments according to the Spirit of God and not according to the flesh. Just as we cannot trust immature children with big responsibilities, the Lord cannot entrust babies in Him with jobs they are incapable of handling.

Yet this does not mean that He will not give beginning Christians responsibilities. He will let them handle situations that they can manage. As parents, we allow our younger children to do small jobs at home under our supervision. However, we would not think of sending them out to handle a business deal for us because they are not old enough and would not have the knowledge to even begin to understand our business.

The Holy Spirit teaches us and trains us to learn God's will and His ways. When we have successfully learned these ways, then He sends us out to perform jobs for Him. Many young converts get into trouble as they are so eager to serve God and have much zeal, but lack God's wisdom and training. They eagerly go out to "save the world," yet have not been groomed by the Holy Spirit. We need to let the Spirit of God engage us in the "school of the Spirit," and let Him tell us when we are ready to go out. When He sends someone forth, He makes a way and provides for them. **Faithful is he that calleth you, who also will do it (1 Thessalonians 5:24).**

Much discredit has been brought on the name of the Lord by eager souls preaching while not even being free from the spirits of pride, poverty, sin and worldly ways. The Lord's method is to first cleanse and train us before sending us out in full-time ministry. This does not mean that we are completely purified before God can use us, nor that we will cease from making mistakes. However, the Lord will have done enough in us for us to be able to handle the ministry to which He has called us. Many times the "call" comes from God several years before the actual sending forth. We see this in the apostle Paul's life (**Galatians 1:13-18**).

Getting back to **Isaiah 9:6**, we see that God relates to us as a child, because He was a child; as a son, because He was a son (He was a teenager); then as a man because He grew to full manhood and took the responsibility of the government on His shoulder. He grew from a child, to the young man, and finally to the mature Son, so He can relate to us on any level we are walking.

The Lord is so close that He can, and does hear us, and He understands us. He came in the form of flesh so He knows how we feel. **Hebrews 4:15-16** says, **For we have not an high priest which cannot be touched with the feeling of our infirmities; but was in all points tempted like as we are, yet without sin. Let us therefore come boldly unto the throne of grace, that we may obtain mercy, and find grace to help in time of need**. In the Greek text, the word *infirmities* means physical or moral weaknesses. From this we can see that the Lord Jesus is a high priest who can "feel" the pain that you and I feel.

If we are hurting, then Jesus is hurting. If our hearts are aching, then His heart is aching. Every time we hurt, He is hurting with us. His heart is grieved over our infirmities. He does not want us to suffer with these things; He wants to help in our time of need. He wants us to be well, joyful and whole. He does not want us to suffer with aches, sorrows and sicknesses.

If we do not find relief after praying and seeking God to remove our suffering, we need to ask God if there is something in our lives that is blocking us from receiving His answer and His peace. We need to ask God what is the root cause of our problem. Many times, the Lord in His wisdom cannot even answer this prayer right away because we are not ready to receive it. So we must be willing to wait for our answer.

Sometimes it is too painful for us to receive a revelation of "self." God has to wait and love and nurture us, and let us grow more before He can give us our answer. We might not be at a place in the Lord where we could deal with our problem, even if we knew the answer. Yet Jesus knows when we are ready to receive. As we come to that place in due time, we will overcome and get the victory. The Bible says in **Ecclesiastes 3:1**, **To every thing there is a season, and a time to every purpose under the heaven.** The Lord can relate to us where we are, whether as a child, a son, or full-grown adult.

Spiritual Immaturity

One of our biggest problems in the body of Christ is that we do not see one another with "spiritual eyes." If we see a Christian that is in an adult body, we often assume they are spiritually full-grown and we treat them that way. On the other hand, we may look at a young person and neglect to consider that they could be a "spiritual adult." **2 Corinthians 5:16-17** says, **Wherefore henceforth know we no man after the flesh: ...Therefore if any man be in Christ, he is a new creature: old things are passed away; behold, all things are become new.**

We look at a person in a woman's body and see a woman instead of the spirit within her, which is made in Christ's image. We see the color of a man's skin with our natural eyes and may fail to see the spiritual man. Many of the ills within the body of Christ today stem from this problem.

If we were walking in the Spirit, this would not be the case. We would see a brother or sister that was immature and acting like a child, and we would treat them as we would our children when they act childish. Instead, the devil often comes against us and we end up fighting with one another, which shows our immaturity also.

We frequently do not want to speak to the people that we have the problem with, so we avoid them, though the Scripture tells us to pray for them, do good to them, and love them. We can act just like little children refusing to speak to one another. If we were adults we would not quit speaking to our children or get so upset. Yet, in the body of Christ, this happens over and over, exposing both sides of the faction as immature.

The mature Christian has learned to let the Lord do his battling and takes a burden of intercession for the offended party. He extends love and mercy.

There is so much division in the body of Christ because there are so many "babies." God wants His children to grow up and quit fighting with their brothers and sisters.

It reveals our immaturity when we fuss and fight, just as natural children do when they are little and have disagreements. We need to let the Father take care of the child that is out of order. We need to make sure we are in order and let the Lord deal with the ones that are not. He is big enough to handle our brothers and sisters who are out of order.

Our position should be to pray for them, love them, and forgive them.

As we mature and grow in the Lord, we come to a place in God very similar to the period of time in our lives that corresponds to the teenage years. We begin to believe we know more than our fathers and mothers, and instead of listening to them, we try our own wings.

Many "teenage" Christians, having discovered some knowledge and truth in God's Word, begin to act as though they know more than all the great teachers of the Word. They learn how to walk in victory in some of the truths, and instead of waiting on God to teach them the rest, they "take off" with a few truths and end up pushing those out of balance. If they would allow the Lord to complete His work in them and send them forth in His time, many problems could be avoided.

"Teenage" Christians many times think they have the answers to everyone's problems. They are out to "set the world on fire." They feel they know it all. They are so eager to do something for God, even if it is the wrong thing. They feel they are ready to assume all the duties of an adult.

Our teenage children in the U.S.A. are so eager to learn to drive an automobile, they beg to drive the car. When they are old enough, we take them to the country and teach them to drive on a dirt road. After they learn to make right turns, left turns, turn around, and back up, they feel they can drive. They exclaim after a few practice sessions, "I can do it now; I can drive."

It is the same way with "teenage" Christians. If the Lord endows them with certain gifts and blessings, or gives them a taste of His power to minister, they feel that they are then ready to go forth and handle the gifts. Obviously, just because our teenagers can drive on the dirt road, we would not immediately turn them loose on the Los Angeles freeways, as they may have a wreck.

So it is with the Lord's dealings. Just because He uses us a few times to minister in the gifts, it does not mean that we can now handle a big ministry. It takes time for the Lord to prepare us for what He has in store for us. It is a process of the Holy Spirit fashioning us. **Philippians 3:21 says, ...Who shall change our vile body, that it may be fashioned like unto his glorious body, according to the working whereby he is able even to subdue all things unto himself.**

When we see "teenage" Christians we should not discourage them, but rather channel their activity in the right direction. We should not dampen their spirits but rather pray for them, love them, and encourage them in the Lord. We all go through our babyhood and childhood before we reach adulthood. We should be as kind to those that are passing through these stages as we would have liked for others to have been to us while we were there. We forget sometimes where we have been.

Spiritual Maturity

There are many "babies" in Christ and many in various other stages but sadly enough, there are few mature Christians. God's ultimate intention is for us to grow into fatherhood, even as Paul and other saints of the New Testament did. We are not to remain babes. The picture of Jesus in **Isaiah 9:6** ends with His taking the government on His shoulder.

How we need saints that will shoulder responsibility in the Kingdom. We have so many "babies" crying to God, "Give me, give me," and "I want, I need," and so few saying, "God, what can I do to help?" We need Christians who will say, "What can I do for you? Lord, do you need me to pray, fast, or endure hardship to get the job done? Do with me as you will!"

In reading **Isaiah 9:6** about Jesus having the government on his shoulder, I have always pictured Jesus as the Good Shepherd with a little injured lamb thrown over his shoulder, carrying it back to the field. One of the functions of His government is to take care of His children.

God is yearning for mature sons to help Him with the lambs. He is looking for those willing to take the burden in prayer and help bind up the wounds of those who are injured. It doesn't matter whether that injury came as a result of someone straying away, or if they were innocently ravished by a wolf. The Lord is looking for mature sons to care for them, not cast them away leaving them in the brambles to die unattended because they have been rebellious. What a beautiful picture of our Lord, the Good Shepherd, who is always concerned about the lost sheep! **Matthew 18:11-12** says, **For the Son of man is come to save that which was lost. How think ye? if a man have an hundred sheep, and one of them be gone astray, doth he not leave the ninety and nine, and goeth into the mountains, and seeketh that which is gone astray?**

We need to have the Good Shepherd's heart also, but so

many times we push the straying lamb over the brink of the cliff. We unkindly say, "Lord, they are just causing problems; they should straighten up or get out." We should not be guilty of this. But the reason we are is that we fail to realize the battle is in the Spirit. We are still trying to battle in the flesh, while the way to get the victory for our brothers and sisters is in the prayer closet, battling in the Spirit (**Ephesians 6:10-18**). We have been given some powerful weapons: prayer, faith, fasting, and many more. The Word of God is our greatest and most powerful weapon and we need to utilize it to overcome the enemy.

Attributes of God

God is eager for us to grow into manhood. When we reach that place in the Lord, we will have the same attributes that our Father has.

What are some of our Father's attributes? **Isaiah 9:6** reveals this as he says, **...his name shall be called Wonderful, Counsellor, The mighty God, The everlasting Father, The Prince of Peace.** A name always reveals something about a person or a product, etc. We make the statement regarding certain people, "He has a good name." A name is synonymous with one's reputation.

In this verse we can see our God referred to as Wonderful! If we had this revelation written within our hearts, we would not doubt the goodness of God, nor would we blame Him for the evil in this world.

I John 3:21 says, **Beloved, if our heart condemn us not, then have we confidence toward God.** Evil was originally meant to be nonexistent. It was meant to exist only as the opposite of good. For evil to exist, it takes an act of someone's will. Some moral being must deliberately choose to disobey the laws of God for evil to exist. If none of us ever broke God's laws or disobeyed, there would be no evil: Evil is the result of a broken law.

Lucifer, who was once an angel created by God as a moral

being, made the first decision to sin and break God's law. Due to his sin, he was cast out of heaven, down to this earth and hell, and a third of God's angels who listened to him were cast out with him. This account is found in **Isaiah 14:12-15**, **Ezekiel 28:12-18**, and **Revelation 12:7-12**. We will not deal with the devil and his evil fallen spirits here, but will cover this in another book, *Exposing Satan's Devices*.

Many people blame God for all the evil in the world today, and do not understand why God would allow it to exist if He is so wonderful and a God of love. If God destroyed all the evil in the world at this moment, it would mean everyone that had evil in their hearts would be destroyed too. God, in His mercy, has chosen not to do this, but instead has given each of us a chance to come to the knowledge of Him and His ways, so that we might become free of our depravity.

Someday (in the not too distant future, according to God's Word) sin and evil will be destroyed at the second coming of the Lord. All that do the works of evil will perish because they have chosen sin instead of receiving the gifts of salvation and deliverance provided for them through the Son of God. God plans to give everyone an opportunity to either accept or reject Him before the end. **Matthew 24:14** says, **And this gospel of the kingdom shall be preached in all the world for a witness unto all nations; and then shall the end come**.

When we see the results of iniquity and evil, it should cause us to turn to God for help and deliverance, instead of blaming Him for all of the bad things in the earth. Many still bring reproach on our Wonderful Saviour by declaring, "Well, God may not be responsible for evil, but He allows it, so that puts Him at the source of it anyhow." The Bible declares otherwise. In **James 1:13-18** we find:

Let no man say when he is tempted, I am tempted of God: for God cannot be tempted with evil, neither tempteth he any man: But every man is tempted, when he is drawn away of his own lust, and enticed. Then when lust hath con-

24

ceived, it bringeth forth sin: and sin, when it is finished, bringeth forth death. Do not err, my beloved brethren. Every good gift and every perfect gift is from above, and cometh down from the Father of lights, with whom is no variableness, neither shadow of turning. Of his own will begat he us with the word of truth, that we should be a kind of first fruits of his creatures.

Everything that is good and perfect is from God, and He is not sending evil. We have allowed evil by choosing to sin, but, praise God, He made a way to for us to overcome it through Jesus.

We are the first fruits of God's Son Jesus; therefore we have the same opportunity to overcome as He did. He overcame death, hell and the grave, and we also can do this by walking in the power and Spirit of the Lord. The Lord declared in **Luke 10:18-19, ...I beheld Satan as lightning fall from heaven. Behold, I give unto you power to tread on serpents and scorpions, and over all the power of the enemy: and nothing shall by any means hurt you.** We do not have to be a victim of Satan and his demons; we can have the power to overcome in the name of Jesus! We can be a "victor" or a "victim"; the choice is up to us. If we choose God and His way, we are promised victory! If we are living in defeat and failure, it is not God's fault; it is our own.

We have been given the Spirit of God within us. This same Spirit raised Christ Jesus from the dead (**Romans 8:11**). And since this power raised Him from the dead, is there anything that He cannot overcome? If He conquered death, cannot the Holy Spirit heal a sick body? deliver a drug addict? set the homosexual free? or give us power over any sin or situation? He is able. We are the ones who have neither sought nor obeyed.

We would much prefer to put the blame on God instead of taking a good look at ourselves, appropriating His power and His way of victory. The Word of God says His name shall be called Wonderful! We need to cry to God to fill us with His love and power. Then we can know Him in all of His wonder!

Our Counselor

God is also called "Counselor." The world is presently spending enormous amounts of money on counselors. People are running to marriage, financial, and psychiatric counselors looking for answers to their problems. As Christians, we have access to the best counsel available.

We have access to the highest wisdom and knowledge in the world through Jesus. As Christians, we forget this fact many times and seek counsel from the wrong sources. There are even Christians that are seeking knowledge through the occult when they should be seeking Jesus. Many are going to fortune-tellers, palmists and spiritualists for their answers. Others are consulting astrology and horoscope charts for guidance and counsel. Most are not aware that by doing this they are opening their spirits to witchcraft influences (**Deuteronomy 18:10-22, Isaiah 8:19-20, Acts 19:18-20**). Christians are suffering from demonic harassment that takes such forms as abnormal fears, nightmares, unusual and tormenting sights and sounds, freak accidents, fatal illnesses and torturous diseases. The root causes of these things can be any type of satanic involvement. The Lord meant for us to seek His counsel, not the devil's nor the world's.

The gifts of the Holy Spirit are one means by which the Lord speaks to His people. He is restoring these neglected gifts that are so needed in the church today such as the true gift of prophecy, the word of knowledge and the word of wisdom (**1 Corinthians 12:8-10**). Since the church has discarded these over the centuries, man has sought the false prophets for their answers. God wants to show us the direction we are to take and to reveal the things that we need to know regarding the future.

These beautiful gifts give us guidance and hope. Hope is almost a forgotten teaching in the church today. We hear a lot about faith and love, but little teaching about hope. The Lord, through true prophets and prophetesses, speaks words to encourage, edify and give His children hope (**Ephesians 4:11-12, Luke 2:36-37, Acts 21:9**). We must have hope for a better day, or the trials and evils around us will overcome us.

The Lord would have us seek those men and women who have godly counsel, so that we won't be ensnared in the traps of the enemy. If we look at our problems, we may feel as if there are no answers to them. They are too enormous, and our lives are so entangled that we see no way out. However, if we look to God, there is no problem too big for Him to solve. Our main objection to turning our problems over to God is that we don't want to do it His way. We either want it done instantly, or we consider His way too hard. We live in an age of instant coffee, instant tea, instant mashed potatoes, and we want instant answers.

God operates by the principles in His Word, so we must line up with those principles if we expect to overcome our problems. For example, if we have financial problems, we need to examine God's Word for what He has to say about financial problems, and then line up with that Word. Are we handling our money wisely? Are we tithing and giving to God's work? Are we lazy or slothful on our job? Are we in debt for our lustful wants? Do we really need the things we buy? Are we wasteful? Are we living for God or for self? Do our money and material possessions belong to God? Are we willing to leave material things behind should God call us to do so? Are we willing to sell all and give to the poor? All of these questions posed here have their answers in God's Word. If we take time to study it and ask God what we need to do to correct our situation, He will show us.

We are usually asked to take one step at a time to correct our situation, as the Lord leads. Then after we have obeyed in that step, He leads us to the next one. We must give the Holy Spirit time to help us straighten up our lives. We did not get into a mess overnight, so it may take some time to get out of it. However, if we will continue to walk in the Lord's counsel, he will correct our situation.

Maybe our problem is a stormy marriage or unruly children.

The Word of God tells us how to correct these problems. Prayer can change any unbearable situation, making all things new in Christ. The key is to follow God's way in solving the problem.

Perhaps the problem is a health problem. Many people are seeking God to heal them but are refusing to change their eating habits or emotional indulgences. Some people have even received healings from God, but have not kept them because they continued to violate His natural laws. If a man was healed of ulcers, yet went back to filling his stomach with everything he wanted to eat with no restraint and still harbored resentment in his heart against others, he could soon have the ulcer again. The symptom may have disappeared for a season but the root cause of the problem remained.

We are seeing the Lord heal many people today only because of His mercy and grace, yet many are not remaining healed. Many then think they really did not get healed after all. This is not true. They just did not take advantage of God's grace by continuing to seek and follow after Him. They never asked God to show them the root cause of the problem. If they had done so, the symptom would have continued to cease and the root cause might have been exposed.

Rebuking symptoms is like pruning branches off a tree. They keep growing back and have to be pruned again.

Some people are habitually in the prayer line. They are prayed for over and over, with no permanent results. The reason for this apparent failure is that they haven't dealt with the root of the problem. **Matthew 3:10** says, **And now also the axe is laid unto the root of the trees: therefore every tree which bringeth not forth good fruit is hewn down, and cast into the fire**. God's mercy and love have trimmed the branches many times to allow us to get to the place where the root problem could be revealed. We need to be grateful for this. We should also remember this when we see others, young in the Lord, who keep coming for prayer over the same problem. They do not need our criticism, but our love and prayers. They may need to grow some more before God deals with the root problem, so He just prunes the branches for awhile.

God wants to show us the underlying cause for our problems. If we are sick, suffering or struggling under the weight of heavy burdens, He wants to release us. **Proverbs 26:2** says, **...the curse causeless shall not come**. If we are suffering under the curse of Satan and this world, there is an underlying cause. Our counselor, Jesus, wants to reveal to us that cause so we can correct it and have the victory in Him!

Our Mighty God

Not only is He our counselor, He is the mighty God! The same God that led Moses and the children of Israel out of Egypt by parting the waters of the mighty Red Sea is still on the throne today. **Hebrews 13:8** says, **Jesus Christ the same yesterday, and to day, and for ever.** He still saves today, heals today, and delivers today! When Jesus paid the price on Calvary for our sins, He declared, **...It is finished...** (**John 19:30**). He finished His mission; it was completed. His death purchased salvation, healing and victory for all. **John 19:17-18** says, **And he bearing his cross went forth into a place called the place of a skull, which is called in the Hebrew Golgotha** (Calvary): **Where they crucified him, and two other with him, on either side one, and Jesus in the midst.** He took the penalty for the sins of not only those standing at the foot of the cross, but also for the sins of all people in all ages. **Isaiah 53:4-6** states: **Surely he hath borne our griefs, and carried our sorrows: yet we did esteem him stricken, smitten of God, and afflicted. But he was wounded for our transgressions, he was bruised for our iniquities: the chastisement of our peace was upon him; and with his stripes we are healed. All we like sheep have gone astray; we have turned every one to his own way; and the Lord hath laid on him the iniquity of us all.** He took our sorrows so we need not be stricken with them. He made a way for us to have peace in our souls. He took stripes on His back so that we do not have to suffer with sickness. He took our hell so we do not have to take it. If we only realized the mighty work He did on the cross! Truly he is a mighty God! He has already done so much for us and continues to show Himself strong on behalf of all who trust Him. If we are living beneath our privileges as Christians, it is not the Lord's fault. He has made provision for us, but we must receive it and walk in it.

A great many of our problems exist because we do not have faith in God. Either we do not trust Him, or we limit Him. The Lord gave my husband Bud the name for this ministry one day while we were in prayer. CHRIST UNLIMITED really expresses the nature of our God! We are not to limit Him. He is a big God! He is more than able. He can do anything! We should not limit Him to our preconceived ideas. Can He only do certain kinds of miracles, while unable to do others? No, our God is unlimited. He not only did miracles, He can do them today.

Although Jesus is not walking our streets today, He has returned in the person of the Holy Spirit, and is still able to perform the same miracles He did when He walked this earth in the flesh. He has not changed; man is the one who has limited Him. The Israelites were guilty of limiting God while they were in the wilderness, and we know the things they suffered because of it. **(Psalm 78:41, Yea, they turned back and tempted God, and limited the Holy One of Israel.)**

If God speaks something to your heart and it seems bigger than your mind can conceive, remember, we have a *Mighty God*! Nothing is too big, neither is anything too small for Him. If your big toe is hurting, He is interested. Now, I know someone will say, "I would not bother God with my big toe." However, God is big enough that it does not "bother" Him when we share our small problems with Him. After all, He took time to number the hairs of our head, and He takes note when even a sparrow falls to the ground. **(Matthew 10:29-30: Art not two sparrows sold for a farthing? and one of them shall not fall on the ground with-**

out your Father. But the very hairs of your head are all numbered.) Our God is a Mighty God who encompasses the small and the large, for in Him things are sizeless. He is an infinite God. He is omnipresent (present in all places at the same time), omniscient (He knows all things), and omnipotent (He has unlimited power and authority). What a mighty God!!

Our Eternal Father

Our God is also the everlasting Father. For many of us, one of the hardest things to comprehend about the Lord is His Father's heart. This should be easy. However, due to a relationship with our earthly father that may not always have been natural and good, we have problems. Human fathers fail us, whereas our heavenly Father cannot fail us. Earthly parents make mistakes, treat us unfairly at times and hurt our feelings. We bring these things over into our relationship with the Lord and see our heavenly Father in the wrong light. We need healing in these areas and if we ask God to heal us, He will.

Many of us have hurts and wounds affecting us today that go back to our childhood. We need not bear these any longer; Jesus wants to heal them. A lot of our bad habits and immature ways stem from our lack of discipline as children. When we finally find the Lord, He has much work to do in us to bring us to the place of complete mastery over self.

The main purpose of the Holy Spirit's work in our lives is to conform us to the image of Jesus Christ. When the Holy Spirit comes in, He begins His work on the flesh and its lusts. We must always yield to the Spirit's work, yet we must be careful not to try and change our old ways through fleshly means. God does not want us to change ourselves, but rather yield to the Holy Spirit and let Him do the changing. He knows what is best for us and just where to begin. If we listen to Him and obey, we shall overcome all the sin and weakness in our lives.

As long as there are certain areas in our lives that are still weak, these are always the target of our enemy, the devil. He attacks us and we find ourselves yielding to him and our flesh. Afterwards, we are sorry that we have failed God and hurt Him. That is when we need a Father we can run to and ask for His forgiveness.

Our heavenly Father is always there with arms outstretched in love. He takes us in those arms, holds us, and says, "It is all right; I understand; I know the spirit is willing, but the flesh is weak." (**Matthew 26:41: Watch and pray, that ye enter not into temptation: the spirit indeed is willing, but the flesh is weak.**) Our Father is there to comfort us and heal the hurt when we disobey through weakness. He helps us and encourages us to keep walking with Him, for He knows that one day we shall be strong like Him.

We will not hinder our walk by unintentional falls if we keep our hearts pure before Him. Praise God, we have a God who has a Father's heart of understanding, and who is always there to help and comfort us. He truly is the everlasting Father. How many times will He help us? He will help us as many times as we have need, providing we really are seeking to follow Him. He will not cast us away for "His mercy endureth forever." It is everlasting. In **Psalm 136** we find twenty-six verses that state, **His mercy endureth forever**.

Our Father is so merciful and kind, and yet many people still believe that it is He who places sickness and disease upon His own children.

We, as natural parents, would be horrified at the thought of afflicting our children with a disease (if we had this power). Yet, our heavenly Father, who is full of mercy, is constantly accused of this. We simply do not know the love of God if we believe this lie of the devil. If God the Father gave up His most priceless possession, His Son Jesus, in order that we might live, how can we possibly imagine Him putting sickness upon us?

Our Father loves us, cares for us, and heals us. Praise God! When we need a Father, He is always there. In some areas of our lives we can fellowship with God as a friend, but until our weak areas are perfected, we need a "daddy." He is truly the everlasting Father.

Jesus, the Prince of Peace

Concluding this study of **Isaiah 9:6**, we see another portrait of God: He is the Prince of Peace. In a world where there is so much talk of peace, there is none. In **Jeremiah 8:11**, we find the statement, **...Peace, peace; when there is no peace**. This is also the cry heard today. There is only one who can offer permanent peace. That one is Jesus.

Upon conversion, one of the first things people often comment about is the new-found peace they have in their hearts. The world is troubled on every side, but in Christ we find peace. Those outside of Him are restless, troubled, anxious, fretful, and full of fear.

The Word of God declares in **Isaiah 57:21, There is no peace, saith my God, to the wicked**. Until we come to the Lord, we never have rest in our hearts. Peace is one of the fruits of the Holy Spirit found in **Galatians 5:22**. When we allow the Holy Spirit to control our lives we walk in perfect peace. **Thou wilt keep him in perfect peace, whose mind is stayed on thee: because he trusteth in thee (Isaiah 26:3)**.

One of our primary difficulties is keeping our minds on the Lord. The devil is always trying to divert us to think carnal thoughts instead of keeping our thoughts in subjection to the Word of God.

How can we be free of worry and anxiety? We must deliberately change our thoughts. We must look to the Lord and ask Him to free us of our fears, and then we must think on things that bring peace.

Finally, brethren, whatsoever things are true, whatsoever things are honest, whatsoever things are just, whatsoever things are pure, whatsoever things are lovely, whatso-

ever things are of good report; if there be any virtue, and if there be any praise, think on these things (Philippians 4:8).

Jesus said in **Matthew 5:9, Blessed are the peacemakers: for they shall be called the children of God**. The Lord not only wants us to know His peace, but also He wants us to distribute His peace.

The body of Christ needs healing and needs those who sow seeds of peace instead of discord. If we want peace in our churches and homes, then we must be the ones who are the peacemakers. If we obey the Lord and walk in His light, His peace will come to our entire family. **And all thy children shall be taught of the Lord; and great shall be the peace of thy children (Isaiah 54:13)**. By following the Prince of Peace, we can bring His peace into our midst.

Why is Jesus referred to as the Prince of Peace? Because God the Father is the King of Peace, therefore His Son is the Prince of Peace.

They are of the Melchizedek order of priests. **For this Melchizedek, king of Salem, priest of the most high God, who met Abraham returning from the slaughter of the kings, and blessed him: To whom also Abraham gave a tenth part of all; first being by interpretation King of righteousness, and after that also King of Salem, which is, King of peace; Without father, without mother, without descent, having neither beginning of days, nor end of life; but made like unto the Son of God; abideth a priest continually (Hebrews 7:1-3)**.

Melchizedek is referred to here as the King of Salem or King of peace. He is a priest without beginning or end, the King of righteousness. Jesus is referred to as the "Son" or "Prince," and Melchizedek is the "Father" or the "King."

Since Abraham paid tithes unto Melchizedek and He has neither beginning nor end of days, we know this is God manifest in the flesh in the Old Testament. He was the high priest then, as Jesus is now our high priest.

When God talked with Adam and Eve in the garden, He

appeared in some visible form, for the Bible records Him walking in the cool of the day. He was not just a spirit who spoke to them. Could it be that this same Melchizedek was there as God manifest? What a glorious priesthood!

We can also enter into Christ's peace and priesthood, if we but follow in His steps. Peace is one of the most beautiful treasures that we inherit from our Lord. Money cannot buy it, but it is free to all who will come unto Him. We can have His peace even in the midst of the storms of life.

To Know God Brings Victory

There are many blessings and attributes of God that have not been dealt with in this book, but as we go on in our walk with the Lord, we will continue to have these and other facets of His nature revealed to us. God's desire is that we get to know Him more and more intimately. We now only have a glimpse of His mercy, compassion, virtue, faith, justice and truth. **We see through a glass, darkly (1 Corinthians 13:12)** as we view His love, patience, meekness, longsuffering, humility, stability, kindness, holiness, and zeal. God's awesomeness is revealed as we discover His vastness, greatness, wisdom, power and severity (this severity being directed toward sin and those that continue in it).

God is a just God and hates sin, but loves the sinner. God is love, and we are grateful for that love. He has so many blessings for those that love Him. He wants us to have them all and will gladly give them to us as we are able to handle them. He longs for mature sons with whom He can share His heart, secrets, revelations and desires. For this to occur, we must first have His nature, love, joy, peace and victory. He does not want us to be continually beset by sin, failure and sickness. He wants us to be free to go and share with a lost and dying world the "good news" about Jesus.

It is my prayer that we would all come to know Him in a deeper way. We now have only a glimmer of what God really looks like, but I pray that our conception of Him will continually come into sharper focus as we see more and more of His true nature. If this divine revelation truly settles in our hearts, there is nothing the devil can do to keep us from going forth victoriously, bringing light and life to others who want to know "what God looks like."

Let us offer this prayer to the Lord: "Father, we come in Jesus' name, thanking You for Your love toward us as mortals. Give us a revelation of Your true nature and character so that we might be able to trust You and follow You at all costs. Let us take this revelation and share it with those that do not know You as a loving God. Lord, let us never blame You for the sin and evil in the world, but rather let us look to our own hearts and allow You to cleanse us of those things that offend You. May we daily walk in more knowledge of You and Your ways. Lord, now I want to pray for my brothers and sisters in You. If they need healing, I ask that You touch them with Your miracle power. You are the mighty God who desires to do good to us, Your children. Bless them and make them whole in spirit, soul and body. In Your name, I pray, Amen."

Index

God, knowing Him 1, 2, 3, 4, 24, 25, 32, 34,
  35, 36
God, no respector of persons 15
God, revealed in Jesus 3
God, seeing Him 5, 6, 9, 10, 11
Goodness of God 8, 23, 25
Growth in the Spirit 7, 8, 14, 16, 17, 19, 20,
  22, 23

H

Hell 6, 24, 25, 30
Holy Spirit 2, 4, 7, 8, 9, 12, 14, 15, 16, 17, 21,
  25, 26, 27, 30, 31, 33
Hope 26, 27

I

Intercession 20

J

Jesus and the lost sheep 22
Jesus, His sacrifice 6, 7

L

Lust for material things 17, 27, 31

M

Maturity 8, 17, 22
Melchizedek, King of Peace 34, 35

N

New birth 7

O

Overcomer, three revelations needed 14
Overcoming 9, 12

P

Peace 14, 23, 29, 33, 34, 35
Power of God 4, 13, 14, 15, 16, 21, 25, 31,
  35, 36
Prayer 8, 15, 16, 19, 22, 23, 28, 35, 36

R

Repentance 4, 8
Root or underlying problem 19, 26, 28, 29

S

Salvation 7, 24, 29
Satan's devices 8, 9

T

Thoughts, controlling 33

W

Word of God 2, 8, 10, 15, 20, 27, 28
Worry, freedom from 33

Additional Books by the Authoress:

Book Titles in the OVERCOMING LIFE SERIES:

PROVE ALL THINGS
THE TRUE GOD
THE WILL OF GOD
KEYS TO THE KINGDOM
EXPOSING SATAN'S DEVICES
HEALING OF THE SPIRIT, SOUL & BODY
NEITHER MALE NOR FEMALE
EXTREMES OR BALANCE?
THE PATHWAY INTO THE OVERCOMER'S WALK

Book Titles in the END TIMES SERIES:

MARK OF GOD OR MARK OF THE BEAST
PERSONAL SPIRITUAL WARFARE

To receive a free catalog of the books, booklets, tracts, computer disks and tapes distributed by Christ Unlimited Ministries, Inc., just send your request to:

Christ Unlimited Ministries, Inc.
P.O. Box 850
Dewey, AZ 86327
U.S.A.

Postnote

The Millers are very glad to receive mail from their readers; however, they are unable to answer the letters personally due the volume of mail that they receive. They will be happy to pray along with their intercessors for all who write with a prayer request; although they do no outside counseling as they believe this should be directed to local pastors as outlined in Scripture.

Christ Unlimited Ministries, Inc. is a non-profit church 501(c) (3) corporation. All contributions are tax deductible. We appreciate your prayers, encouragement and support. Your purchase of this book makes it possible for us to share free copies of Bibles, teaching literature, tracts and downloadable audio/video materials with ministers in third world countries who would otherwise not be able to purchase them.

The Lord gave the word: great was the company of those that published it (Psalm 68:11).

For Additional Study

This book is taken from a course of Bible studies called the Overcoming Life Series. The entire series is a virtual "spiritual tool chest," as it covers a multitude of subjects every Christian faces in his walk with God. It also answers questions that many believers have concerning the current move of God. These are dealt with in a balanced approach and in the light of the Scripture. God's people are not to live frustrated, defeated lives, but rather they are to be victorious overcomers! Other books available with their companion workbooks are:

PROVE ALL THINGS - Christ warned that great deception would be one of the signs of the end times. In this book, instruction is given on how to recognize false prophets and teachings. Clear Scriptural guidelines are given on discerning the Spirit of truth versus the spirit of error. The book deals with how to judge without being judgmental.

THE TRUE GOD - This is a teaching on the character of God, explaining why God does certain things, and why it is against His nature to do other things. It differentiates between the things for which God is responsible and the things for which the devil is responsible. Our responsibility as Christians destined to overcome is made clear so that we can live victorious lives.

THE WILL OF GOD - This lesson teaches us not only how to know the will of God in our personal lives, family, ministry and finances, but also brings understanding as to why God allows sin, sickness and suffering in the world. As overcomers, Christians are not to suffer under many of the things we have accepted as normal.

KEYS TO THE KINGDOM - Instruction on how to gain authority in God's Kingdom through prayer is the topic of this book. Many principles and methods of prayer are covered, such as praying in the Spirit, fasting and prayer, travailing prayer, praise, intercession and spiritual warfare.

EXPOSING SATAN'S DEVICES - This book is a powerful expose' of Satan's tricks, tactics and lies. Cult and Occultic methods and groups are listed so Christians can detect their activity. Demon activity is discussed and deliverance and casting out demons is dealt with in detail. Satan's kingdom is uncovered and the Christian is taught to overcome through spiritual discernment and warfare.

HEALING OF THE SPIRIT, SOUL AND BODY - This book teaches how to overcome emotional problems, as well as physical ones, and how to receive divine healing. It also teaches how to renew the carnal mind and walk in the spirit of life, thereby overcoming depression, loneliness and fear.

NEITHER MALE NOR FEMALE - What is the woman's role in the church and home? Who is a woman's spiritual head and covering? Does God call women to the five-fold ministry? What does God's Word say about divorce, celibacy and choosing a marriage partner? These and other woman related topics are Scripturally examined.

EXTREMES OR BALANCE? - Many Christians have hurt the cause of Christ through "out-of-balance" teachings and demonstrations. This book shows how to avoid those areas. It also deals wisely with the excesses and extremes in the body of Christ.

THE PATHWAY INTO THE OVERCOMER'S WALK - This book contains answers to the questions an overcomer faces as he presses toward the prize of the high calling in Christ Jesus. How can we be conformed to the image of Christ? How does the Holy Spirit work with the overcomers in the end times? What are the overcomer's rewards?

PERSONAL SPIRITUAL WARFARE - Explains the invisible world of spiritual forces that influence our lives and how good can prevail over the evil around us as we prepare for the new kingdom age that is coming. This book will help you overcome problems in your finances, marriage, the emotional pressures of fear, anger and hurt. Here are the keys to victory through spiritual warfare.

MARK OF GOD OR MARK OF THE BEAST - Much has been written and said about the mark of the beast, but little has been said about the mark of God. What does the 666 mean and what is this mysterious mark? How is it linked to the world of finance? Has this mark already begun? This book answers many questions about the mark of the beast and the mark of God, and how they affect Christians.

Write for catalog with pricing for books & companion workbooks plus cassette tapes. We also have electronic books and a condensed Home Bible School on computer diskettes.

Purpose and Vision

> Go ye therefore, and teach all nations, baptizing them in the name of the Father, and of the Son, and of the Holy Ghost: Teaching them to observe all things whatsoever I have commanded you: and, lo, I am with you alway, even unto the end of the world. Amen.
>
> **Matthew 28:19,20**

Christ Unlimited is not "another denomination," sect, or just a separate group. It is an arm of the Body of Christ — the Church of Jesus Christ, which has been called to strengthen the Body at large. We also believe we have been called to help establish the Kingdom of God in the earth.

Christ Unlimited is involved with all Bible-believing Christians regardless of their church or denominational affiliations and committed to helping wherever possible in evangelistic and teaching outreaches.

Christ Unlimited believes that time is running out and the Gospel has not been preached to every creature. Many nations have not heard the Gospel, and in many places, doors for evangelism are closing. We believe it is time all Christians cooperated with the Lord in breaking down denominational walls for a united front line against the kingdom of darkness and in setting up the Kingdom of the Lord Jesus Christ by the power of the Holy Spirit.

Christ Unlimited provides such tools as to enable the saints of God to establish the Kingdom of God in the earth. We encourage groups of prayer warriors who will pray, fast, and intercede for the nations. This, we believe, is weapon number one. We teach believers how to overcome through spiritual warfare and through knowing how to use their authority in Christ Jesus through the Word and the power of the Holy Spirit.

Christians need to know how to bring down the forces of darkness in their own lives and in the lives of those to whom they minister. We provide such tools as Bibles, literature, Christ Unlimited books, and an online prayer ministry. We publish the Gospel going forth via any means of communication, including the innet and videos, as well as literature. We have teaching seminars, Bible schools, and correspondence courses, all aimed at winning souls to Christ and building the Body of Christ into maturity.

Bud and Betty Miller serve the Lord together as founders of the multi-visioned ministry outreach, Christ Unlimited. The outreaches of this ministry have stemmed from a tremendous desire to see the Word of God taught in its balanced entirety. The Millers are firm believers in prayer and, through prayer, have seen many released from the bondages of fear, failure, and defeat.

The outreaches of Christ Unlimited are in obedience to the words of our Lord in **Mark 16:15**: **Go ye into all the world and preach the gospel to every creature.** This mandate from the Lord presents a challenge to our generation as an estimated 25 percent of the world's population still have not heard the Good News of Jesus Christ.

Christ Unlimited Ministries also is dedicated to teaching God's Word. **Hosea 4:6** says: **My people are destroyed for lack of knowledge.** Many Christians are leading defeated lives simply because they do not know God's Word in its fullest.

Christ Unlimited Ministries has provided for those who desire to know God's Word in a greater way. The main thrust of the teaching and literature is directed at "How to be an overcomer." In the endtimes, we must be prepared to overcome the onslaughts of Satan. Many Christians are suffering needlessly, because they do not know how to overcome sickness, depression, divorce, fear, and financial failure. Christ Unlimited Ministries provides answers for troubled families as well as trains workers for service.

www.ingramcontent.com/pod-product-compliance
Lightning Source LLC
Chambersburg PA
CBHW020952030426
42339CB00004B/65